BE THE CHANGE in the World

Lisa Dalrymple

Crabtree Publishing Company
www.crabtreebooks.com

Author
Lisa Dalrymple

Publishing plan research and development
Reagan Miller

Editor
Anastasia Suen

Proofreader and Indexer
Wendy Scavuzzo

Design
Samara Parent

Front Cover:
Alamy: Neil Cooper (bkgd)
Thinkstock: boy in front

Photo research
Tammy McGarr

**Production coordinator
and prepress technician**
Tammy McGarr

Print coordinator
Katherine Berti

Photographs
OneWorld Schoolhouse Foundation: p. 13, 15, 17 (b), 18, 19 (br)
Ryan's Well Foundation: p 8
Shutterstock: Charlie Edward: p. 4; nui7711: p. 7 (b); De Visu p. 12 (b); a katz: p. 21 (t); Vira Mylyan-Monastyrska: p. 21 (b); spirit of america: p. 22
Wikimedia Commons: Public Domain p. 5
All other images by Shutterstock

Library and Archives Canada Cataloguing in Publication

Dalrymple, Lisa, author
     Be the change in the world / Lisa Dalrymple.

 (Be the change)
Includes index.
Issued in print and electronic formats.
ISBN 978-0-7787-0622-9 (bound).--ISBN 978-0-7787-0634-2 (pbk.).--
ISBN 978-1-4271-7609-7 (pdf).--ISBN 978-1-4271-7605-9 (html)

       1. Humanitarian assistance--Juvenile literature. 2. Disaster
relief--Juvenile literature. 3. Voluntarism--Juvenile literature. I. Title.

HV553.D35 2014   j363.34'8   C2014-903838-0
                                           C2014-903839-9

Library of Congress Cataloging-in-Publication Data

Dalrymple, Lisa.
  Be the change in the world / Lisa Dalrymple.
       pages cm. -- (Be the change!)
  Includes index.
   ISBN 978-0-7787-0622-9 (reinforced library binding) -- ISBN 978-0-7787-0634-2
(pbk.) -- ISBN 978-1-4271-7609-7 (electronic pdf) -- ISBN (invalid) 978-1-4271-7605-9
(electronic html)
  1. Social action--Juvenile literature. 2. Young volunteers--Juvenile literature. 3. Social
problems--Juvenile literature. I. Title.

  HN18.3.D354 2015
  361.3'7--dc23

                                    2014032613

Crabtree Publishing Company

Printed in Canada/102014/EF20140925

www.crabtreebooks.com   1-800-387-7650

Published in Canada
Crabtree Publishing
616 Welland Ave.
St. Catharines, Ontario
L2M 5V6

Published in the United States
Crabtree Publishing
PMB 59051
350 Fifth Avenue, 59th Floor
New York, New York 10118

Published in the United Kingdom
Crabtree Publishing
Maritime House
Basin Road North, Hove
BN41 1WR

Published in Australia
Crabtree Publishing
3 Charles Street
Coburg North
VIC 3058

Contents

Beliefs, thoughts, and actions

Gandhi was a world leader who believed in kindness, fairness, and peace. He saw many things in the world that were unfair. For example, in some countries, girls do not have the same **rights** as boys. Sometimes people think they have to accept things they know are unfair. Gandhi believed you should do something to change those things. He stood up for others. He worked to make changes in peaceful ways.

A girl cares for her sister instead of going to school.

Gandhi's message was to "be the change you wish to see in the world." Even one small action can make a big difference. By acting to make the world a better place, you can be the change, too!

Gandhi lived long ago. People remember his message today.

MAKING CHANGE HAPPEN!

What does Gandhi's message mean to you?

5

We are the world

There are billions of people in the world. Your house and your school are part of a local **community**. We are all part of a **global community**, too.

Our global community connects us with people in many countries. We can get fruit from Brazil and read news from England. The Internet helps us communicate with people everywhere.

Change in one place can affect the whole world. Cancer research in one country helps patients everywhere. An oil spill pollutes water in many countries. In a global community, one person's actions can affect people around the world. You can be the change in the world.

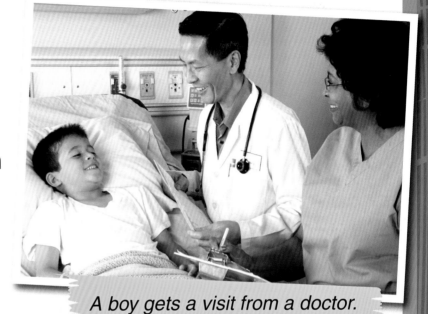
A boy gets a visit from a doctor.

An oil spill in Thailand harms the environment.

7

Well done!

Ryan has raised money to build wells in more than 15 countries.

Anyone can make a positive change! Ryan Hreljac was only six years old when he found a **cause** that was important to him.

NAME:
Ryan Hreljac
(say "Hurl-jack")

FROM: Kemptville, Ontario, Canada

CAUSE: Bringing clean water to those in need

Making change!

Ryan was in grade one when his teacher taught his class that some places in the world did not have clean drinking water. The polluted water was making thousands of children sick. Some children were even dying. A well would bring clean water to people who needed it. Ryan decided to take action. He made a plan to earn money to build a well. He did extra chores and talked to other people who helped raise money, too. One year later, Ryan had enough money to build a well in Uganda, a poor country in Africa. Ryan's cause grew into an organization called Ryan's Well Foundation. Together, Ryan and his foundation continue to build water wells in countries all over the world.

What would you change?

Ideas for change can come from anywhere. Like Ryan, you might be at school when you learn about a problem. Or you could be at an after-school club. You might read about a problem in a book or see something on TV.

Think about what is important to you. Talk to your friends and family and brainstorm ways you can work together to make a positive change.

Miguel is good at public speaking. He makes speeches about recycling.

Ashanti likes fundraising. She makes money selling lemonade, then donates it to disaster relief.

Carla is a good knitter. She makes scarves for families in need.

MAKING CHANGE HAPPEN!

How can you find a problem you can change? Ask yourself:

- What do you like to do?
- What are you good at?
- How can you use your skills to help others?

Getting ready!

Once you find a problem, learn as much about it as you can.

Students in Australia read more about the problem they have found.

Abraham does research on the Internet.

You can also find an organization that is making a change. Ask how you can help. What is needed most? How many people need help? How can you learn more about the problem?

Children in Ecuador get information from a volunteer.

Maria asked herself these questions:

What change do I want to make? I want to help kids in St. Lucia whose schools were damaged by hurricanes.

Why is this important to me? Those students have no books, but my school has many.

What can I do? I will run a book drive.

Who can help me? My friends, teachers, parents, and OneWorld Schoolhouse.

Books being delivered in St. Lucia.

MAKING CHANGE HAPPEN!

What change do you want to make?

What can you do?

Make an action plan!

An **action plan** helps you to decide what steps you need to take to reach your goal. It helps everyone who is helping know what they need to do, too. When everyone works together, your actions will make the biggest change!

MAKING CHANGE HAPPEN!

What is the goal of your action plan?

Maria's Book Drive Action Plan

Goal: Collect books for Soufrière Primary School in St. Lucia

When: November 14 to November 30

Where: In the hall outside our classroom

Who: Students in Ms. Stack's class

What is needed: Boxes, tape, posters

Students pack boxes of books to send to St. Lucia.

Students in St. Lucia carry books to their classrooms.

15

3-2-1...action!

It's time to see the change in action!

November 5 Put up posters for our book drive.

November 6 Call newspaper to let them know about our book drive.

November 7 Send a letter asking families to collect gently used books to donate.

November 12 Make an announcement. Remind students to bring in books.

November 14-30 Collect books at recess and lunch. Pack books into boxes.

December 3 OneWorld Schoolhouse will pick up books.

Support Our

BOOK DRIVE

November 14-30

Outside Ms. Stack's class

Bring in your gently loved books for kids in St. Lucia

Don't give up!

Remember, sometimes things happen that you can't plan for. Maria should not be upset if she collects fewer books than she had hoped. She should remember why her change is important. It's okay to try again and ask for more help!

The sign outside Maria's school

Central Public School

PLEASE SUPPORT OUR ONEWORLD BOOK DRIVE NOV 14-30

MAKING CHANGE HAPPEN!

Who will you ask to help with your project?

What will you need to do?

Share it! Celebrate it!

Loading books into a truck in Canada

Share the story of the change you made. Let people know about your success. For example, Maria can tell people how many books she collected. Thank everyone who helped you or donated. Share your pictures and your good feelings!

It's important to tell your friends, your community, and people at your school about your success. People might decide to help in the future. Your story may **inspire** others to make their own changes, too! The world will become a better place one change at a time.

The books arrive in St. Lucia.

Share your success by...

Sending a story to your local newspaper.

THE NEWS

Students at Central PS Collect 37 Boxes of Books for Students in St. Lucia!

Telling everyone over the announcements at school.

Creating a scrapbook to show off your notes, photos, and news clippings.

Making a presentation to your school or community.

Making thank-you cards for everyone who helped.

Think about it!

You did an amazing thing! It's important to take a moment and think about the value of your actions. Being the change takes hard work, courage, and **compassion**. You made your global community a better place.

Ask yourself:

- How did it feel to help people?
- What did you learn about yourself?
- What did you learn about other people in the world?
- What part of your project worked well?
- Is there anything you would do differently?

Hurray! You did it!.

Remember, you can find ways to help change the world at anytime and anywhere. Be ready!

Danielle delivers food for hurricane relief.

Ethan volunteers at an animal shelter.

MAKING CHANGE HAPPEN!

How will you keep up the good work? Will you run a book drive every year? Or will you find a new way to be the change?

Help others! Help yourself!

It's a big world, but we are all connected. When you make a change, you are making things better for everyone, everywhere. Did you know that helping others can help you, too? Imagine if people everywhere worked to make the world a better place!

Every single person can be the change!

Helping others gives you a chance to:

- try new things
- make new friends
- use your skills in a new way

- learn that you can solve problems
- inspire others to be the change
- make the world you live in a better place!

A change anywhere in your global community can help change the world! You can inspire everyone to be the change that makes the world a better place to live.

Learning more

Websites

www.ryanswell.ca Learn more about Ryan Hreljac and Ryan's Well Foundation.

www.earthskids.com/welcome.aspx Read about issues that affect our local and global communities and how kids can change the world.

www.kiwaniskids.org/en/KKids/Serve/Planning_a_service_project.aspx For step-by-step instructions on how to plan a project, including useful tools and tips, visit Kiwanis Kids.

Volunteer organizations

www.oneworldschoolhouse.org OneWorld Schoolhouse helps Canadian students send books to students in the Caribbean.

www.rainforestofreading.org Young readers may be interested in their Rainforest of Reading website.

www.littlewomenforlittlewomen.com Little Women for Little Women in Afghanistan, started by Alaina Podmorow, works to support the education of girls in Afghanistan through fundraising and creating awareness about equality, freedom, and peace.

www.freethechildren.com Free the Children was created by Craig Kielburger to help stop child labor in the world.

Books

Fullerton, Alma. *A Good Trade*. Pajama, 2013

Leist, Christina. *Jack the Bear*. Simply Read, 2009

Shoveller, Herb. *Ryan and Jimmy: And the Well in Africa That Brought Them Together*. Kids Can, 2008

Words to know

action plan (AK-shuhn plan) noun A list of steps that must be taken to complete a task

cause (KAWZ) noun A reason for action; something to support

community (kuh-MYOO-ni-tee) noun A group of people living in an area, who often have similar interests

compassion (cuhm-PASH-uhn) noun A feeling of sympathy for others in distress and a strong desire to help

global community (GLOH-buhl kuh-MYOO-ni-tee) noun The people of the world connected by similar needs and cooperating to share resources such as clean water, air, and food

inspire (in-SPAHYUHR) verb To encourage positive feelings in someone, making that person want to take action

organization (awr-guh-nuh-ZEY-shuhn) noun An association or group of people working together for a purpose

rights (RAHYTS) noun Things that a person should be allowed to have, get, or do

A noun is a person, place, or thing. A verb is an action word that tells you what someone or something does.

Index